Nixes Mate Review

Anthology 2016-17

Nixes Mate Books
Allston, Massachusetts

Copyright © 2017

Edited by Annie Pluto, Michael McInnis
& Philip Borenstein

Book design by d'Entremont
Cover photo from the collection of Lauren Leja

All rights reserved. This book or any portion thereof may not be reproduced or used in any manner whatsoever without the express written permission of the publisher except for the use of brief quotations in a book review or scholarly journal.

ISBN 978-0-9991882-5-5

Nixes Mate Books
POBox 1179
Allston, MA 02134
nixesmate.pub/books

Nixes Mate *is a navigational hazard in Boston Harbor where, during the Colonial period, pirates and mutineers were gibbeted .*

Contents

Buckshot Words	Bart Solarczyk	1
Fog Window	Belinda Subraman	2
my vagina is a battleax	Heidi Blakeslee	4
Girl Poetry	Heidi Blakeslee	6
Opposition	Gloria Mindock	8
Transcript from Lucy Ricardo's Therapy Session (#1)	Taylor Liljegren	10
Transcript from Lucy Ricardo's Therapy Session (#2)	Taylor Liljegren	11
Transcript from Lucy Ricardo's Therapy Session (#3)	Taylor Liljegren	12
Alchemy	R.M. Engelhardt	14
Month Mouth Moth	Dan Raphael	16
Tristesse	Howie Good	17
My Dirty Life and Times	Howie Good	18
Mermaids of the Charles River	Lee	19
Seduction	Clare Martin	34
The Neighbors	Nancy Iannucci	36
Taxis to Nowhere	Nancy Iannucci	37
Pomegranate Explosion	Richard King Perkins II	38
The World's Fattest Man	Corey Mesler	40

Perfectionist	Robert Beveridge	42
Love Notes	Aden Thomas	43
Active Art Is Always Overhead	Ron Androla	44
what one meant to do	Mark Young	47
Winter Rental	Mark DeCarteret	48
August	S.E. Clark	50
Helen	S. E. Clark	52
Beauty Sits at the Table	Tim Suermondt	53
Earhart's Blackbox	Sam Landry	54
The First Time We Had Sex, We Got Sweaty &	Megan Bell	56
I live on a Finger Lake now	Megan Bell	58
Death Trip	Kurt Nimmo	60
In a Deserted Farmhouse	Richard D. Houff	62
The Chosen People	Elissa Rashkin	64
Kaddish for Chantal	Elissa Rashkin	66
Burning Leaves	Daniel Fitzpatrick	69
Winter Days	Mark Jackley	70
Alchemy	Seth Jani	71
No Sanctum	Catherine Arra	72

Water Aerobics | Catherine Arra	74
Sister | Emma Johnson-Rivard	77
Vietnam Memorial III | Zvi A. Sesling	80
Black Moon | Zvi A. Sesling	82
Waterslides in Auxiliary Hospital Washroom | Daniel Thompson	83
Misguided Pathos | Angela Dragani	90
Medium of Release | Michael Istvan	94
Swan | Natalie Crick	102
Bosch & Keaton Hide Behind a Poem About a Deer | Jim Zola	103
A Fire Without Light #493 | Darren Demaree	104
A Fire Without Light #494 | Darren Demaree	105
A Fire Without Light #495 | Darren Demaree	106
Forward | James Croal Jackson	107
Glass Alibi | Charles Kell	108
Summer is a Dream | Gary Sokolow	109
recipes | Mark Young	110
Near Miss | Robert Stout	112
Dear Ron | Bart Solarczyk	113

Nixes Mate Review

Anthology 2016-17

Buckshot Words | Bart Solarczyk

I'm not a crook
not a sniper

just a poet
with poor aim

buckshot words
blasted in a world

where nothing's
worth stealing.

Fog Window | Belinda Subraman

I accept my strangeness
big loves faded

memories spill
on a messy desk

disbelieving all
that could be my cane

anxiety kaleidoscopes
wet voltage
knowing excites
dreams in a river

the idea of India
is taffy in the bend
of a warm spiced pull

memories warp into mood
belief in all stages

time is weather

life is a water-color
of angels in the rain

my vagina is a battleax
Heidi Blakeslee

an old battered ship
that is said to have once
sailed in grandeur

pressed velour flags flying
amidst sea birds

a treasure chest
in the hull

pirate boys scrubbing the decks

a maiden at the helm
looking out towards
the bow spirit

shined and oiled wood
on the quarter deck

a proudly driven vessel once,
now aimless
afloat in a sea of fog

a rusty anchor waiting to sink
into the cold
depths
of sea weed

forgotten

Girl Poetry | Heidi Blakeslee

they probably
think

oh, girl poetry,
great
it'll be another one
about flowers
or kissing
or periods
or vaginas
or staring longingly at someone

but in reality
we write about
the streets

freedom to speak
spoken words that ripple
through cool air
like bullets

women write hard
against the spite

spines of books creased
from heavy reading
heavy petting
not mentioned
here

women write about whatever shit
is real
that's why
when a woman reads
a good poem
there is a whoosh of silence
at the end

a skipped second
where everyone is forced
to say

damn

Opposition | Gloria Mindock

anna pavlova twirled danced on point gracefully but was angry at her leading man but not to worry stephen king to her rescue with heavy eyebrows he shot skunks onto the stage squirting perfume into the stage floorboards while chewing tobacco pavlova legs suddenly grew and were like wings kicking those who hated her so one night 50,000 legs fell on the stage during the performance and stephen stood there patient laughing evil watching people fall hurt at midnight those bodies were in front of trains waiting to be crushed like when he was a child witnessing a friends death by train choo choo choo anna and stephen sat on a bar stool and drank stephen was in recovery no more anna with an imagination like stephen laughing showing how her delicate facial expression changed as she collected exotic birds and animals and then bit them one by one teeth bloody growling mean wanting more parrots angry ballerina with rage and stephen smiled to see another carrie born with doors slamming exorcist head and many legs forming their own dance company called the dying swans fragile but with a kick a royale beating job jete

jete vole ballerina vole and as you do stephen starts his
next story but anna did not like this she wanted a better
ending jete jete jete flying into the air with perfect
balance the air air air held her up floating majestically
conservative seeing a double image doppelganger her
eyes were bloody hands raw and around 3:00 everything
she bit walked the earth bones of crawl stephen retired
in maine where he lives now and he thinks of his anna
as he looks out the window sees all the bones roam in
the yard calling to him calling to anna as if revenge
would help dark night low shiny moon skunk perfumes
his porch floor boards phew phew phew

Transcript from Lucy Ricardo's Therapy Session (#1) | Taylor Liljegren

I think I'd like to talk about what is grey.

About chocolate and arroz con pollo. About my husbands hands; how they smacked and sounded against a soft stretch of skin the moment I began to love him. About the censors, the just lip kisses, our beds: parallel plots. About the baby. The "How?"(as if there wasn't the kitchen counter after dinner dishes, the damp bathroom floor before showering). About the way my Mother is always looking slightly above my eyes when she speaks to me. Calls him Mickey. Hates the ride to see us. About my best friend; Her "No" as "Yes." About broomsticks sounding against ceilings and grapes between your toes. About my closet, my costume. My pins and polish. The henna rinse. The lip stick. And all the other ways I have chose to be without being.

Transcript from Lucy Ricardo's Therapy Session (#2) | Taylor Liljegren

Last night, I dreamed the man I love ironed
my heart out flat across the kitchen counter.
Wrote out his ink-dark love for me across all four
chambers, gave it back blanched on a bed of satin –
a valentine. All schoolyard. All paste and puncture.

I grew grey at the absence. The walls lost all color.

Next, laughter: first soft from the farthest stretch of the
room then sharp –
        broken plates, forks and knives hitting floor,
tea kettle cackle –

I was outside of myself then.
He held me in his hand so easy,
so Morning Paper,
so Baseball.

I was my own gift, and I said "thank you" to the open
wound between my breasts

Transcript from Lucy Ricardo's Therapy Session (#3) | Taylor Liljegren

Someone once said that insanity was doing the same thing over and over while expecting a different result.

I think this person must have been a man.
I think this person must have had a wife who wanted too big.

I want to tell you about early morning. When the lights aren't up yet. When I lean my body out the window into the thick soup of the city, and everything is, again, just beginning.

This is the moment right before the Wish:
When he walks in about to say something
that will shatter me.

The plan before the punch line.
The air a thrown pie sails through. The dark you sit in as the spotlight searches for your skin
(When you are nearly nothing, when your heart is not a

poem or a symbol or a theme song –
but an organ, that is heavy and mostly tired.)

This is bringing teaspoon to pursed lips.
The sharp intake before the unraveling,
When I want to weep,
but wail.

Alchemy | R.M. Engelhardt

There is no thing said between the moments

Complete & unshaken whose voice remains

For the sake of determination.

Mind you, this is truth without the lethargic séance

Of years, mind you
That these are the words of

Hypocrites and players, dreamers & fools who would
Assume or consume your heart with their

"Things"

Calculate and transcend the towering dooms of doom
Love & cherish all faces equally at the mere

Mention of sirens or hollow men
For beauty is a butterfly up in a tree or quite possibly

The sound of one devoted heart, not a superman

Nor a super model nor the uncontented cries of

Oversexed rock stars.

Time will do quite fine

Without them when time knows what desire

Beholds between the moments & the distance of

"Years"

Month Mouth Moth | Dan Raphael

From midnight to midnights not always 24
When we had 6 fingers on each hand
One egg for each hour
When the thumb could wrap all around the pinky
With 6 no fingers in the middle
                                        Yes a thumb is a finger
What if we were double jointed and the fingers could fold either way
Delicate handshakes   organic gloves   all in it together

A body calendar:
Yearning with 12 mouths, 30 teeth each, on average
Depending on the light, as if a window but couldn't be
3 walls tween me and outside
A train   a torpedo   a refrigerator box

Tristesse | Howie Good

If you heard the Kalashnikovs firing on surplus workers, you gave no sign. You just glanced one way, then the other, before passing inside. It's possible, even likely, that you experienced a delayed reaction, a kind of thunderstorm blue. You wondered aloud which famous rock star you were. Everything is art, you claimed, including the 20-minute headstand you do on your terrace each morning. Later, when your date arrived wearing a lovely dress of used tinfoil, she asked, "What made you want to look up 'tristesse'?" You wouldn't say it was the snakes and turtles that someone had dropped from a great height, but it was.

My Dirty Life and Times
Howie Good

Impossible tasks attract me,
It's good to create obstacles.

I, at least, don't work well
without obstacles, To bring

the past back to the present,
the noises must become music.

The rest is telepathy.

Assembled from Robert Bresson, Bresson on Bresson, Interviews 1943-1983, and Notes on the Cinematograph

Mermaids of the Charles River
Lee Okan

She heard them calling, calling for her the weeks leading up to the first spring blooms. Their voices faint, submerged beneath a ceiling of ice, yet she heard them singing, calling for her. She imagined they said her name, entombed in their calls. The rollicking waves rocked below the bridge as she trudged through the snow. It became like slush, caking the pedestrian walkway on the Harvard Bridge, and here, she heard them sing loudest. She paused, here, where they sang the loudest: were they singing for her? In the morning on her way to work, their voices burst above frosted waters, and at night, on her way home, the voices sang lullabies good-bye to the day. Their voices sank, then faded beneath the surf.

Nerissa crossed the Harvard Bridge twice a day, swarthed in scarves and bundled in wool. She heard the voices through her headphones, over the trilling piano keys, the rhapsodies and harmonies. She heard the voices asking, persuading her to join them. Nerissa walked on. In her office in the Pru on the fortieth floor, she heard the voices calling, a soft hum rumbling in her veins. She turned her eyes out over the river, stretching from Harvard to the head, and lowered her eyes away from the calling, persistent calling, longing thronging calling her to come.

Was it home they called her to? The flood of sleep immersed her into dreams, and in these rambling dreams, tempests broke across the land, with rain, with water rising high and intending to catch her inside the foamy waves. Nerissa tousled her blonde hair away as she moved back towards her desk cluttered with charts and reports, and as she pushed a strand from her face, wiped the squalor dreams from her mind.

Her eyes fell away from the Esplanade banking the shores of the river, the tree-lined strip of haunts and spirits who arose at night, gallivanting with homeless moonshine and motley clothes. The crew teams, the sailboats were missing from the icy river today. On warmer days, on windy days, the sails would dapple the water with color and the little rowboats would steady towards the river's head, rounding just beyond the bend and into the harbor. In the harbor, the cruise ships departed hourly from the Long Wharf, to the Navy Yard or to Hull, Hingham, and Quincy; down past to Cape Cod and Provincetown. She had once traveled so far, to the tip of the sleeping fisherman, the very end of Massachusetts. She had stood at the end of the world, looking east, across the ocean and to the Old World.

From the Old World and from the Orient, great ships arrived in mid-July. The ships, they came again, for Fleet Week, and families and friends waited on the harbor to watch them come in one after another, great white ships blasting triumphant horns.

She remembered she had waited too, among the crowd, pressing in upon her and hot. Lowering her sunglasses, she peeked above the rim; something stirred within her. They lifted their faces upwards and the sailors looked down, grinning wide, corn-fed teeth, dressed all in white. They came down the planks with duffle bags thrown over their backs, and their medals shone and sparkled gold. In mid-July, the sailors came, moving three or four abreast down the sidewalk streets.

She watched them in Copley Square, sitting around the fountain pool while the children splashed and played, and the dogs panted with feet dipped in the water. The sailors dressed in white, moving three or four abreast down the sidewalk streets, down Newbury and through the Garden, and she hesitated and watched them go in white.

In July, it was a delusion to think of mid-winter. Now, there was sunshine aplenty and bodies nearly naked in the white sand. For forever it seemed, and she hoped. She would often drive down to Nantasket Beach alone and sit to read and waste away the weekend hours. They called to her then, they always did, but the sun was warm and she was so full of life, she whispered back, "I do not want to go just yet." The Paragon Carousel rotated to mournful songs on the boardwalk of pastel colored buildings, the last vestige of Hull's Golden Age.

She remembered the sailors moving three or four abreast down Boylston Street, and the solemn one detached from the others. He floated away from them and settled on the edges of the Copley Square Fountain, while the others followed the tortoise and the hare to stained glass and the Trinity Church. He took off his sharp shoes and rolled down his socks, and dipped his pale, colorless feet into the water.

She hesitated and watched him from above the edges of her book. The voices ever present, and the birds sang Greek; she hesitated and watched him from above the edges of her book. His medals gleamed, polished for show, and he turned his straw-colored head to the voices of his friends, waving him over by the doors of the church. They beckoned, and he remained, catching her eye as she closed the book.

She had once traveled so far, to the tip of the sleeping fisherman, the very end of the world, looking east, across the ocean and to the Old World. It would be summertime again: she would skip and dance, sheathed in nothing more than flimsy film and gauze. In July, the ships would come again, warmth and effulgent light. She remembered, she remembered. Dancing away from him towards the ebbing flow of the ocean water on Race Point Beach in the summer. They came early to catch the sunrise. Their distant voices hummed on the edge of the horizon, near the ripples made by breaching whales. She asked Levant, "Do you hear them, too?"

"Hear what?" He asked with a brazen smile. His voice was so flat and sweet and she could taste the Vermont apple orchard on his breath as she turned away from his kiss to the voices.

It was only the ocean, and she beckoned him with outstretched arms, saying, "Come, come follow me into the water."

She heard them singing, each to each, but ignored the voices waking from the foam. She beckoned to Levant and caught him in her arms. "I don't think two people could have been happier than we," she said, and to the waters, to the voices calling one to another, she thought, "Not yet, you will not have me yet."

Levant stayed a week, and in that time, they went everywhere together. It was summer; she took off from work, and climbed the cool blue spiral tower towards the top of the fish tank. They stared down over the rim, at the sea turtle wavering through the green-blue water. The barracudas darted between the sloping walls of coral, and the stingrays waltzed and dithered near the bottom. She never did this; she never had time. Nerissa cast a glance to her lover, took his hand and softened. The reef fish darted and splayed, and one detached from another to float along the belly of a nurse shark. Levant pointed to the moray eels, and she counted the tiny sea turtles.

Through the dark rooms, the eerie rooms echoing with children's laughter and teenager voices, they gazed into the windows of sea dragons and moon jellyfish, the gaping mouths of piranhas, the hidden octopi, orange and iridescent against the Pacific coral.

After, they crossed the Seaport Boulevard and sat on the steps at the ICA. She said, "Let us go then, you and I, to Castle Isle…" and so they went by taxi later that night to Castle Island in Pleasure Bay, where the Tories and the Royalists once absconded. It was dark, and the evening spread out across the sky. She heard the voices on the crashing waves and the birds singing in Greek. He felt her tremble beside him; he worried after her pale face. To him, she whispered, "Let us go, then, you and I…" She took his hand and led him forth.

They walked down the Head Island Causeway, which took them out into the ocean with insidious intent. It was a narrow strip of road, a path rising out of the water, and as it curved, there at the center of the horseshoe, a pavilion sat empty and beckoned.

"Let's rest," she said to Levant, and as she motioned to the benches, he spun her around and kissed her. Kissed her, and she felt the rush and light inside her as she pressed her lips to his. Fireworks went off around the Boston Harbor, celebrating the ships return, the sailors, the happy weather of July.

The shells burst orange and pink over the city. A few large comet stars erupted, extending large tendrils that whipped out in either direction. A few fish explosions; he and she watched the flaming debris swarming in random directions, twinkling, fading yellow on the backs of the eyes. They watched the fireworks, the sad dazzling display. She counted down the moments now that they reached the mid-point of the week. Each second she savored, clamoring after time, begging it to last a little bit more. In three days, Levant would depart. And she watched her lover tenderly, fidgeted, looking back and forth from the fireworks to her. Their eyes met, and they fell in love. "I don't want to go just yet…" Levant was saying, but the fireworks ended, and she grew cold. Time slipped away and then they moved forward on the Head Island Causeway towards the star-shaped fort. The island dark and empty, they kissed in abandon among the shadows on the sloping lawn, the fireworks cracking, whistling, blasting above them.

They had once traveled so far, to Race Point Beach to catch the sunrise, and swarthed in blankets, they waited on cold, white sands as the sky glimmered pink and orange. In July, the ships would come again, he said, and in the meantime, he would write to her, he would call her. Their voices hummed distantly on the edge of the horizon; she had not forgotten them. "Please. I hope you will…," she said, dusting the sand off his pant leg. He wrapped her up in the blankets, in his embrace. "Do you hear them, too, calling each to each?"

"The whales?" He asked, looking off on the horizon.

She smiled. "Yes, the whales…" Of course, she thought, those are the voices, and the birds do not sing in Greek.

They woke into the warmth of early afternoon, and she swooped over him to plant a kiss on his forehead. "I do not think two people could have been happier than we," she brushed his sandy, straw-colored hair from his face. "Oh, Levant, none happier."

They stripped to their skivvies and dashed down the beach towards the water. She beckoned to him with outstretched arms, saying, "Come, come follow me into the water."

The water was warm and the air was warm, and they bathed their bodies in the dark blue waters. It was only they upon the beach that afternoon, only their blankets and clothes spread out across the sand, scattered in a path towards the waves.

They played at being fish, diving down into the depths. Nerissa opened her eyes and looked up towards the elusive ceiling, the filmy effulgence of the sun washing out the world above. She heard them sharply and so distinctly, singing each to each. Calling her name, calling her to come. Their voices haunted the twitch of seaweed floating near her hand, encircling upon her arm, and it called so sweetly, so much louder than before. The rollicking waves may rock the world above as the whales broke through to the surface and roared, but here the world was calm and here the world serene.

She saw them riding heavenward on the vortexes of waves. They gathered the salt bubbles and beaded them on Maiden Hair tendrils green. Wreathed in seaweed red and brown, the sea-girls beckoned and brought her down. They grabbed her foot and held her tight, and laughed a little more to see her dear. Nerissa finally saw the voices that had called her for so long, combing back their white hair with seashells. All dimples, smiles and curls, complexions green and white, they beckoned her more with outstretched hands, and Nerissa looked up once more to the drowning, to the fading, to the dimming light.

Their voices sank, then faded beneath the surf, and she fell down with them.

She heard them calling, calling for her the weeks leading up to the first spring blooms. Their voices faint and submerged beneath a ceiling of ice, yet she heard them singing, calling for her. She imagined they said her name, imbedded in their calls. The rollicking waves rocked below the bridge as she trudged through the snow. It became like slush, caking the pedestrian walkway on the Harvard Bridge, and here, she heard them sing loudest. In the morning on her way to work, their voices burst above frosted waters, and at night, on her way home, the voices sang lullabies good-bye to the day, and their voices sank, then faded beneath the surf.

But then a pale, colorless hand outstretched from nowhere and brought her up. She rose and rose and rose with the hand, guiding her up to the watery ceiling, until she, like the whales, broke the surface and breathed. She breathed and breathed again, panting as her hand clutched her throat, and the roaring in her ears overcame the singing, the fading singing, the longing thronging fading down below.

Levant looked worried, but with a brazen smile, he said, "I thought I lost you, and we just met." Nerissa looked at her feet paddling beneath her, thinking, Not yet, no, not yet.

Not yet would the tidal waves claim her. The flooding dreams, the tempest at nights no longer bothered her. She listened to him talk about the Orient, her sailor Levant, brushing his straw-colored hair from his face as he lay in her lap. They were on Nantasket Beach, the antique carousel turning to the chiming music. The week was drawing to an end, and her sailor Levant talked about the places he would go, the places he would sail. He tasted like Vermont, syrup and apples when she kissed his lips.

"When I finish, we should sail down the Eastern Atlantic Seaboard," he said. "I'm serious," Levant said, shading his eyes from the sun.

She dipped her head in front of his face to block the light. "So am I."

"Would you then, travel with me? From Maine to Florida."

"Why stop there? We could go to Cuba, too. Find the mermaids in the Gulf of Mexico."

"Why stop there?" Levant challenged, flashing his corn-fed white teeth. Her eyes widened momentarily at his sincerity. You and I, she thought. Nerissa linked her arm in Levant and they braved their faces towards the sea, against the wind, against the sun.

They talked about spending a year after his service sailing, the boat they would buy, the things they would need. Nerissa would quit her job; she would sublet her apartment; she would follow the sailor wherever he traveled.

"I'll write you every day," he said, "I'll call you when I can. Will you wait until next July?"

Nerissa looked up and out across the water; she heard them singing, heard their sirens, calling and calling for her to join them. But her sadness had ebbed away because of this straw-haired sailor. She turned her face back to Levant, "I will."

She remembered it all, nearly nine months ago in July, underneath the starry sky, the evening spread out and wonderful, filled with bursts of orange and pink. But it was winter now, and she trudged to work over snowy paths, and below the bridge, the voices shrill, the voices unquiet, sang to her to come.

She heard them singing, each to each, and calling her for weeks leading up to the first spring blooms. It snowed, it snowed, it snowed every day, and she soldiered on in gloves and scarves, great down jackets, moving through the caked snow. In her office in the Pru, she heard them as she prepared herself to journey home.

It so happened news came from the Orient of a ship that went down. What was the error, what was the cause? How many survivors arose from the foam and swam for the shore? The weeks leading up to the early spring day were silent of news, and then, a name, a face, a memory. She whispered, "Levant, I do not think two people could have been happier than we," before moving out in the winter squall.

Was it home they called her to? She remembered the day she almost drowned at Race Point Beach, the calm and serene depths, what a pleasure they had been. Her dreams were filled with rising water and foamy waves, and the voices calling her, calling her to come.

As she came to the Harvard Bridge, she heard them loudest, nearest to her heart. Their voices burst above the frosted waters; they pleaded and they called. She saw them riding on the surfs of waves, their coral necklaces orange and pink against their green and white complexions. They were all dimples and smiles and curls, and as she neared the center of the bridge, they beckoned more with outstretched hands.

At the 182.2 smoot line, she hesitated and watched. Beneath the crusts of ice, she saw them there waiting. Nerissa looked up once more to the fading light around her, nearly dusk, and all orange and purple and black. A few people on the other side of the bridge wandered by, and a few on her side, wandered off in the distance.

It was time, then, to say good-bye. They had called her long enough, and he was already beneath the waters. She could join him yet. She had waited, she had waited. July again would never come. They had called and beseeched her, and finally persuaded her, and she decided it was time. Nerissa took off her coat and her scarves and her hat, she stepped a naked, pale foot into the snow. Breathing a moment, she gripped the green railing and looked over Boston.

From Harvard to the head, her eyes fell away from the Esplanade and rounding just beyond the bend, into the harbor. And from the harbor to the ferries, departing to the Long Wharf, the Navy Yard, to Castle Island, farther on to Hull, Hingham, and Quincy, to Cape Cod, Provincetown and Race Point Beach. She had once traveled so far, to the tip of the sleeping fisherman fishing for scod and cod cheeks from the Atlantic oceans. She had stood at the end of the world, looking east to the Old World.

Now, she gripped the green railing once more and fell to the sea-side girls wreathed with seaweed red and brown. She heard the voices loud and shrill, singing still; she thought of Levant, she thought, None happier than we, and then she drowned.

Seduction | Clare Martin

Each bone is a highway. Each organ's a town on the map of the body.

What is the nameless city you have taken me to? In it, we reside in a junked motel. There is dust from the road in my mouth when you bend to kiss me for the first time, again.

I have played a pair of deuces, all in. I have set the path behind me on fire.
I've lived one black dream after another for this one desire. Once, twice to love – who knew?

Is it a miracle, or a dilemma of death?
You bite my tongue softly; blood-tang sweet. Take me into a blissful prison. You fall asleep with the .45 under the pillow.

The bathroom door hangs off hinges. Ice melts in a cracked bucket. Neon light blisters threadbare curtains.

All night it is like the sun is watching. I decide to believe God doesn't exist but such belief is ineffectual. How else would I have breathed so long outside of your arms?

The Neighbors | Nancy Iannucci

Mother's mood
swings four seasons.
Father's forest fire rages.
Son doesn't set.
Daughter's paisley dress
goads them in a dance.
Pulling down the shade,
their sideshow closes
for the evening.

Taxis to Nowhere | Nancy Iannucci

I have to go! I have to go where I feel most happy &
right now   here   isn't it. IT is _____
(depending on his fixation, IT could be Italy, Florida,
California to name a few). He staggered into the taxi &
gave me a reassuring wink with one of his black eyes.
We watched him clutch a brown paper bag so taut I
couldn't help but think of Linus & his blue blanket.
Funny, he was cast as Charlie Brown in his eighth-
grade school play. He reached down to scratch his left
ankle bloated with a sandwich bag of secret Sweetarts. I
knew he was checking to make sure it was still there.
I'm alright! I won't do anything stupid. Believe me. As
the taxi sped off for the third time in two days, we
turned toward the house like zombies.

Pomegranate Explosion
Richard King Perkins II

Golden copper descends
from the latest sunset

indirectly upon you
lighting contours indescribably seen.

Someday,
we'll dissociate like the forgotten tail
of a falling star

but tonight, our moisture circulates
without resistance, petals on pond water,

drawn together with the ease
of ghost attraction and subtle enchantments.

Smiles and your eyes begin so many things;
fingers curl to secure them

and then –
a pomegranate explosion luminesces
on the endless horizon

and a new sun appears beside us

or perhaps,
with the wish of a lover's whisper,
we have made it suddenly appear.

The World's Fattest Man
Corey Mesler

I was a young sylph. I
was clueless.
I had 50 cents and I
paid to see him.
We were led in a semi-
circle trudge round his
seat. Not three feet
from me, his face
was indifferent, perhaps
masking contempt.
I was shamed. I
knew we were
the freaks; we wanted to
see something worse
than us, more animal,
more meat. I went
home and my mother
had left a cake out on
the counter, multi-

tiered and beautiful,
like a castle, like
fairy tale fare: dark,
mysterious, transformative.

Perfectionist | Robert Beveridge

Seven scars across one arm
six across the other
blade tip rectifies asymmetry

Love Notes | Aden Thomas

Along the highway
just above the cottonwoods

a flock of geese bend
across the blank page of sunset.

Their cursive wings
hover a moment in the salmon light.

You take my hand,
and with your fingers,

you trace our secret language
across the lifeline of my palm.

Active Art Is Always Overhead
Ron Androla

Thin
brush-
stroke
clouds
expand
the ribs
of a drenched
watercolor
sky split like a
barge's
wake.
2 southern
cloud-
streams
penetrate
atmosphere
with their
penile bull-horns
made of chopped

wet rocks,

moist dawn fog,
& tenuous moments of fleshy
veiny northern
dusk. Mountains
of discarded
skulls spit &
blow flames,
apocalyptic
confetti, fanged
lightning
bugs, &
quantum-
shifting
UFOs.
I whittle a confused,
phosphorous-rich,
match-stick head of
tadpole sperm
into a microscopic
knife
that stabs
& guts & pulls blackberry-
bloody
summer

ripples
overhead;
the ripples undo
the pulse & the
breath of me,
they cut wide
holes out of
Lake Erie's
trout-shimmering
surface reflection
trimmed
in old
peach
light;
what
stays
evening,
what's old,

evaporates.

what one meant to do
Mark Young

Please
send a picture &
indicate your
geographical
location. I think
I've just strained
my left arm but
would like to
know more.

Winter Rental | Mark DeCarteret

After backlogging last week's losses
I lob the whole book into the sea.
You could easily see me from any window
but the one in the kitchen with the niche
beneath the sill you have hidden your secrets.
Retired, I shape putty into the littlest of whales
and laugh as the cat swipes at them, riveted
while you pull out your apron like a safety net,
knuckles scored from the table's edge,
before grabbing for the spyglass
keeping look out for that barge
with its belly of paper scraps, parables.
I can taste brine, a billion lies going bad
but this too is garbage, ad-libbed on the deck.
A military jet passes, a red X on its chest,
a gray similar to all the black and white
ever compromised, made to play nice,
its shrill cry a baby hawk's or a ghoul's.
You're wondering if it's still possible
to drown under miles of words,
stirring only to sit even further inside

the British, floor model, version of yourself.
Is it there that you touch the one thing
that serves only your soul, the non-existent?
I feel slipshod and blowsy just mentioning it,
my teeth and tongue bent on my throat,
wanting none of this pinned on them.

August | S.E. Clark

The church bells ring each hour,
of every day in this city.
I hear them most often in Spring and Fall,
and on rare days in August when the sea
grants us a reprieve.
A breeze that tastes vaguely of salt.

They ring in tune with cicadas,
shedding their old skins.

In August, we fry.
By the noontime bell, it's too hot to sit outside,
and the flies will dive at your eyes looking for
a drop of water.
Persistent things;
not even an atom bomb could kill them.

My father told me once, as we ate ice cream
on our porch,
that on blue days in August he looks out at the city
past steeples and skyscrapers;

wonders if he'll be unlucky enough to see the first flash of
nuclear fission.

We would only be unlucky for a second, he says.
We would never see the mushroom cloud.

The files would probably survive.
And maybe the cicadas, too,
singing their canticles under
a detonated sun.

Helen | S. E. Clark

I envy the women in
your pictures
how they put their hands
in your hair
and smile.

They are always
more beautiful than I am;
all your choices rest between
goddesses.

All I have to give you is
my love.

And my love is not
your golden apple
to barter away
to women who will
never hunger as I do.

Beauty Sits at the Table
Tim Suermondt

Acting aloof
   like beauty often does. We,
who are far less beautiful,
   buzz around like bees in front of It,
vying for Its affection.
   It knows we won't get anywhere, we
know we won't get anywhere, but we
   keep trying until Beauty stands up
and walks away, so beautifully of course.
   In the opposite direction we
begin filing out, experienced, battered
   refugees of love whom you can count
on to keep coming back.

Earhart's Blackbox
Sam Landry

Seagulls fly out to dive.
In Indiana our birds can block out the sun
if you're standing right below one
as it takes a step up from the dirt –
little specks of earth and worm, bolts
wiggled off, bits of scrap from who-knows-what
pelt your scrunched up face,
leaving welts and the occasional gash.
I took one of these hawks for a spin
out past the waterfront.
I stopped at a few nice places,
and passed by a couple more:
Rio de Janeiro, Cape Town, New Delhi,
Lae, the Nukumanu Islands.
They toss chum
for famous foreigners.

The Islands are long gone.
I took a conch shell with me,

grabbed it on the way by.
It is sitting in my bag,
but I can hear it in my headphones,
the only reception I get
is a small breeze
that blows my hair over my eyes
as I lay under an umbrella,
sipping on a glass of water
as I discuss aviation with a colleague.

The glass dissipates.
A giant 'E' sits in the dash.
Darling, enough with engineering,
the blueprints are for shit.
Behind us sits an incline
and out there?
Southern California,
Sydney for the lost.

The First Time We Had Sex, We Got Sweaty & | Megan Bell

We laughed. The sky fissured
with wet heat. A hot tongue.
Tonguing the inside of our heads. Am I correct
about the date? Every day
with you unfolds into the outlines of
origami animals taken apart. Yes, even
a few dogs. I need at least one around. Eyes
floating on the lake. Eyes filled with birds.
We are standing dripping
on the interstices of winter & spring. Comfortable
already, with silences. It took so long to arrive.
Our whole lives, even. Our whole bodies.
Climbing down a scaffolding of trauma.
Meeting up, with ideas. The same thing happening
on different planets.
There aren't yet words. I've heard of this
happening before. A systemic synesthesia.
The way your presence
releases into my blood.

The only porn I watch anymore
is amateur stuff. Imagining our bodies
where their bodies are: wings
spread, visceral architecture
flooding, trying
to write down
how the smell of latex transforms
into coffee in the morning you made us – your hands
on my ass,
into the lilac bushes that grew
    next to each of our childhood homes.

I live on a Finger Lake now
Megan Bell

I.
I unintentionally fall out of
attraction with a guy into 'watersports'.
He had emetophobia, anxiety
about vomiting, of other people
vomiting, of what comes out
of the body
during the whole excruciating process. The implications
of what is happening. He thinks
it has something to do with something
he can't clearly remember from childhood.
No, I never

got pissed on.

My father
cannot get out of bed, & Mom's at work. I ask
if he minds if I empty
his drainage bag, & he says, you're not gonna puke

are ya   he sounds

so tired & I say,
no, Dad. I force a laugh
sort of like a cough.

II.
I vomit blood into the lake
and feel better. I bike thirty-three miles
in the pitch black, only
closing my eyes twice. The stars wind
up underneath my feet. Narrative fails
each of us again. Timelines fray,
coming apart. Dissolution framed in softness. Do you ever
just dissolve? Infidelity accusations
before the thought, ever —
then I do it.   I go

bowling every Sunday night in a pool of orange light.
In a memory, I did not suck. In fact, I helped.
I live on a Finger Lake now.

Death Trip | Kurt Nimmo

On the
southern end of Jornada del Muerto
the car radio tells me
China is threatening to start a war.
I wear sunglasses
and drive the speed limit.
East of the Doña Ana Mountains
and up over the San Augustin Pass
they have a missile testing range
and an air force base.
I live inside
a huge yet invisible bull's eye.
If the crazy people
in Beijing and Washington
decide to start a war
over who owns a body of water
on the other side of the planet
there is a good chance
my wife and I will
be reduced to vapor
along with everybody else.

She sits next to me
poking on her phone.
She has no idea the world is about to end.
I reach down and push a radio button.
Yummy Yummy Yummy
by the Ohio Express.
My wife makes a face.

In a Deserted Farmhouse
Richard D. Houff

We stumbled upon a patch of trees
surrounded by tall prairie grass that reclaimed
the clapboard home, and ventured inside to explore.

We found a Victorian winged-back couch
and nothing more as we moved from room to room.

On a dare to descend into a dark root cellar,
there were no takers from our group.

Although heavily armed with squirrel rifles
and shotguns from a day of hunting rabbits;
we all had our hidden fears, and ghost trouble
was at the top for each and every one.

Deserted farm homes were scattered
throughout the county, and in our limited travels;
we had rummaged through several on previous outings.

Everyone that we knew had heard of government controlled

farming, but very few within our domain understood
the outcome of losing one's sense of place.

It all hit home one day
at a farm auction our family attended.

Watching the personal belongings of those affected
on the auction block; I felt a growing sense of despair.

Stripped and abandoned, I couldn't help wonder
what would become of them.

A neighbor within earshot said, that they would probably
head west on Hwy. 16 looking for work; maybe end up
in some California factory doing assembly.

Nobody knew for sure what became of folks
out on the road, but over a three year period,
I watched a steady migration of friends and neighbors
take part in this growing ritual.

No one ever returned, and few kept in contact.

And then one day it was my turn to join
the procession among the lost.

The Chosen People | Elissa Rashkin

They say the grandfather
used to spit on the ground
each day when he passed
the synagogue.
Reluctant fruit
of the rabbinical tree.

Hatred makes no fine distinctions.
A Jew is a Jew and the devil will have his due:
G-d closed his eyes
the army came
and tossed the bodies
into a common grave.
One brother crawled out, broke
in pieces, to tell the story.
The family fled to Romania. The black waters
failed to recede. I wake up

each night

barely breathing

in my broken brother's body
trying
to claw our way out

Kaddish for Chantal
Elissa Rashkin

Art begets art
as sorrow begets sorrow

If there had been no Godard
If we had never sat in darkness
suddenly dazzled
by luminous oceans
and the thin air
of motionless
contemplation

If Karina and Belmondo
had never set foot
on that imagined island
if Jean-Paul's thumb had never
swept across
his lips
to brush away the dust of cinema
to build anew

If there had been no Auschwitz
no six million flames extinguished;
what other memories would our blood carry
like hidden poison

if the mother's tasks had been undertaken
in utter silence
without the camera's caress
would we understand love
without its absence

if each object
reproduced itself in miniature to enter the eye
if there were no camera obscura
if a woman had never dared
to gaze upon another
retaining the imprint on the retina
her gestures

not forced
to look away
if we had never received this gift
of light and shadow
Chantal

Sorrow begets sorrow
the kitchen, the bed, the screen
the tenderness of orphans
the making and unmaking of graven images
then the last unmaking
turns out to be sacrosanct

Burning Leaves | Daniel Fitzpatrick

All October the tall grass
bent northward, uphill,
its ochreous pallor eliding the moonlight
as sun swelled and burst in the thinning oaks.

Then you walked through our Elysium,
your horned feet softened on the quartz,
and as you passed into a shadeless place,
the juncoes (snowbirds, you said)
scattered your ashes.

We'll spend the winter burning leaves,
raking black cautery across the packed hill.
Otherwise the grass will drown
and the deer will ghost to livelier woods.

Winter Days | Mark Jackley

they vanish into cracks
thin as calendar pages real
pages antiquated
as a flint axe

Alchemy | Seth Jani

The forest is everywhere
Like someone's lung blown
Inside out by a largening wind,
A red corolla emerging from
The mouth,
Becoming a place for bees,
The dangerous work
Of transmuting honey out of air.
We circulate in that stream.
Our whole lives beautifully
Stitched and heathered
By the expelled breath
of trees.

No Sanctum | Catherine Arra

I.

From the crown of an abandoned shell

the one no one wanted for the gift shop
the seaside memento; its flawed chamber etched
and cracked, a sliver shattered from its spire
cast aside, masked in muddied mulch, forgotten
until excavated, knocked, shaken
knocked again

the young gecko cascades to concrete
with wet sand, stunned still.

II.

One-eyed heron spindle legs the cloistered courtyard
her haven now, abandoned by the flock, never to mate
navigating her half world, half blind.

III.

Fragile is each thread unwound, unbound
isolated without shape, form, purpose:
twigs in a nest, cells of a hive,
people in democracy divided.

Water Aerobics | Catherine Arra

Four women stomping
down pool laps
cajole the Bistro owner to pipe
out the music – LOUD.
I forget the book.

Big woman
with the biggest voice starts it.
Her entourage in varying degrees
of size and volume pipe in
telling tales
about that first lay; drunken legs straddling
young buttocks
in backseats, closets, cornfields.

60-somethings
loving themselves young.

Then in unison, no cues
the white visor, straw hat
black cap and pink turban

pick up step with the beat,
punch air, singing Rockin' Robin.

We're all rockin' bare toes keeping time.
Man next to me shakes his head
gives up on the Sunday Times, leaves
as they jump, midriffs bulging and
shout, Tequila!

Someone on the ladder shouts back
"No, margarita!"

It's that mix – that zeitgeist
between 1955 and '75
the cold war and Vietnam

when
What it is ain't exactly clear

When we
fought the law…

needed
Help, a Dream Lover, a Dream

It was
The Time of the Season to Give Peace…

Take a load off...

Singin'
…sha la, la la dee dah

Do you remember when we used to…?

Just like that.

Sister | Emma Johnson-Rivard

She wrote a story about two girls in love
talking on a cliff
but never showed anyone.
Wrote another instead
about a murdered boy
covered in wax, this
won praise for its gravity
There was a line about sinking
and she wrote the same cliff in the murder that
the young lovers awkwardly confessed on

The murderer, incidentally
never said a word
He was caught by fate
science conspired against him
She wrote him unkindly, then
was told he had great depth

This is what we call irony.

She went to a wedding, was mistaken

for the bride's sister,
did not dance at the reception
She took a peacock feather for a gift
broke it in half, stuck it in her hair
It was not whole but it was hers

Later, this was not said:
You would not come if I married
You would not dance or
smile for my wife for the sole reason that
she would be
my wife

Both of them are writers, this
is not said
She keeps the feather in a book, is not surprised
when the marriage goes wrong
Her sister, who is not really her sister
has always been an optimist

She returns to the murder story
the one where the dead boy rises
ten years later
preserved in wax
to haunt the cliff side

where the two lovers
young girls with black hair once held hands
and cast stones
across the river below

Vietnam Memorial III
Zvi A. Sesling

The Vietnam Memorial of Maya Lin
is a giant mirror where the living and
the dead seem to intermingle
— Murray Dewart

Whose face do you see – son
or brother crying as you are

Sorrow on a day of sunshine
that cannot warm the heart

The name reminds he is a
son or brother gone forever

The face in the mirror is there
and though the heart breaks

Both leave with an imperceptible
smile at having seen the departed

*Note: The epigraph by sculptor Murray Dewart is
found on Page 21 in his Introduction of Poems About
Sculpture, in "Everyman's Library Pocket Poets"*

Black Moon | Zvi A. Sesling

The moon is black
howlers and creepers stalk
cemeteries and roadsides

The living avoid these places
even animals wary of the ghoul
awaiting by-pass

These islands of horror
even the ghost of your father
gives it wide berth

Waterslides in Auxiliary Hospital Washroom | Daniel Thompson

I'm on the topside of the slide. In the throat, at the threshold of revelation, making an inventory of everything I see. Mineral deposits in the sink, loud graffiti on the walls. Urinal cakes emit the chemical scent of agent-orange flowers. There's one fogged up window, a small toilet stall and three large tubes where urinals should be, wide enough to crawl through, to sit upright, to kneel, like the ones that vent air in hospitals, rise out of the roof and bend at right angles in the open air.

Flowing through corridors of familiar institutions. A toilet flushes in another part of the building. The sound draws nearer, impossibly close, trickling down the inside of my skull. I put my ear to the wall. Water falls along the long axis of my body and passes through the floor, dragging my bladder, seized in an uncontrollable urge to urinate. I step foot forward toward one of the tubes, tugging at my waistband in preparation of a flood.

Threading consciousness through the eye of a needle

poked myself to see if I'm alive and bled; it's the game over threat of living my final life. I can't remember anything too specific. There's a game we play in there. Its name incommunicable and keeps us coming back to find it. Once inside it's easy to forget where I am. I come and go as I please, but never stay in either place for long. Commanding attention to bring information back with great effort to recall, contents of a room itemized in the dark behind eyes, before eyes, how they evolved in response to other eyes because there's something out there watching us. Detects me beyond the threshold, across the placenta-like partition wall.

Waterslides in auxiliary hospital washroom, the janitor rushes in, tries to stop me. Wants me to pay a toll. I put my hand in my pocket. Feel the small, hard shapes of coins fizzle into non-existence like seltzer tablets. "I don't have any money," hands held out, palms up, universal sign for no money, but he keeps coming. Blue dickies morphing into form-fitting policeman's blues, big black boots rapidly outstripping the size of his feet sinking into a grid of floor tiles as the room closes in, curling into n-dimensional space (anything above 4 presenting difficulties to physical objects so accustomed to occupying the more or less flat Euclidian plane) some kind of hyper-dimensional construct experiencing a break down or contradiction, as in the same matter occupying the same space. The skin of reality come peeling off to reveal the operations behind smooth exterior walls made more permeable to waves, light. The whole building, save for the roof, visible from any point inside or out, openwork steel girders bowed like the struts of a barrel or cask. While what should be the static, immovable fixtures of an institutional washroom – mirror, urinal, stall – shift with every angle of my approach, disappearing and appearing halfway up the wall and on into velvety darkness; the limit of programmable space. Blacked out to hide the deep structure of things I am used to seeing (or not seeing) here inside the box. Not even objects or shapes, just atoms, bonded in electrical night: the dark interior of a machine's head tuned to a quiet station, nothing, not even cosmic background radiation nothing. 'Nothing' as far as I can conceive of nothing, but that may be something to something else, unable to raise my eyes higher than the top of the wall and the drop ceiling.

Footsteps echo in layered delay of no-time, hard and wet; assumes a grating, industrial sound.

The janitor reaches out to grab me.

I give him the slip – slide through one of the tubes.

Pop out in the poplar grove.

Behind the mirror is a room. A screen hanging from the roof displays the poplar grove in two-dimensional interactive computer game interface from the eighties. Something watches the screen, images of me as a stick man strolling through the knit graphics of a softwood forest. Flame leaves forever on the verge of exploding into pure colour. Tandem-walking on two legs, dragging my shadow, lagging along behind me.

Trees thin out to a field of tall grass. I wade through with swimming motions of my arms, sweeping the ground for rocks, holes, obstacles in my path. Emerging at the edge of a precipice where I join or am joined by, 'the teacher'. Manipulating the environment through metaphors. Parallax prospectus of mental pictures pro specere the future. Flipping through photographs held up to the sky, taken from different angles, heights, POV of a bird in flight.

Sky spout.

Rainbow waterfalls from spout in the sky, wellspring at headwaters of cloud pitcher pouring milk through cleft columns where sky meets earth. Beading off leaves and rocks finding fissures contiguous through cracked and uneven slabs of stone. Flowing in the dark undetected until it bursts forth into the worn crease of a stream, rushing toward the heart – center of the mandala. Shared affinity with municipal drains, crossed X streams, the one taking on the burden of the other, burrowing into habitat for humanity; the dank basement of a house built into the side of the mountain.

I feel around in the dark. The cave is dry, just the water sloshing inside my skin suit.

Old haunts.

Nobody home. No home should be without a body and nobody without a home. Our bodies and homes are the same sort of thing. Temporary, we're always moving on. When the second little pig moved out he bought a bundle of sticks and built a house.

The house teeters on the edge of its foundations as if the ground will open up and swallow it. House with the false bottom, digging down; further excavations reveal damp grottos, a parking garage, a skeleton beneath the floor. No one can recapture the psychosis of that place. No one is willing to go to such lengths. Enough to scare even ghosts away. Those with a propensity for such things might call it haunted: the house that haunts the town, the house that haunts itself. A long legacy with the realty company, defunct, de-fucto heap of rubble driving down the value of houses around it, hedges raised to block it from view.

Wake up… and the tragedy that befalls me is my folly. If I were an animal what would it be?

Sheep. I sleep, enough. Counting. It's time. Wasted.

I want to wake up in a past locus of time, as a child crying in a twilit room, mom and dad rushing in to tell me it's alright, that it was only a dream, not a clock or a bomb about to go off…

The radio chirps 6:30 bluebird world report Pacific-standard-time to wake-up. Snoozing through news, weather, traffic, sports. Just over one million civilians… did I hear that or was it part of a dream? I turn off the radio, but the voice is still there. Could be the stereo? No. Must be the fillings in my teeth.

I search the house, haunting, hunting for a place without reception, but it's hard to find a spot with no signal at all. Data floating around in the cloud until I hit the right place like watching home movies of myself tottering around a destroyed room, camera shifting amoungst the rubble, solastagia in condemned homes so we can't move out or away. A ghost with no choice of which places to haunt, magnetized to a system of leys free of hunger, disease; supplied only with what a ghost needs, to relive old memories, pine and long for in autochthonic recursion of seasons – resurging streams, recurring dreams.

I crouch in a corner beneath a tall tropical plant.

The chattering stops, but I'm left without a voice in my head.

Just waking up? You should be hearing alarm bells.

If I am to keep this story going I will need to say a few things, otherwise I will roll over and go back to sleep.

Our lives online, games to kill time, games about killing. Blinking, cursor, ready… now there's a game, its name a secret. Ticket, a token, I took the ride. The stub left in my hand spelling out the last few letters of the word, the name of the game – the other half of the story.

Misguided Pathos | Angela Dragani

Please don't tell me you know how I feel.
You – with your murmured sweet nothings,
your Great Uncle's cousin's sister and her ill-defined
troubles.

Your face so alarmed as you desperately struggle
to see my long-familiar self, my eyes, my heart -
And yet peer past my left shoulder with vague feelings
of unease.

It's okay. I really do get it. I was cool,
but now I'm something new and alien,
and quite possibly dangerous.

Please don't tell me how I should feel.
You – Ha! You who have never tasted that burning
      metal spit
while the wind steals your breath and you pluck the
stars from the sky.

Dancing on dew in that secret ethereal forest,
and the colours! Oh man those colours in a million
 billion hues
and every single one a promise and a possibility.

Please don't tell me how to fix myself, I'm not broken.
You – who have always been on a first name basis with
 your sanity,
never felt that creeping, clinging otherness.

That hostile stranger,
That malevolent bastard,
Felt him wrapping you in black in a room that only
locks from the inside.

Trapped with him for days, weeks, months,
while he feasts until there is nothing left.
Staying alive loses all appeal and there is only the cold
 black left.
Please don't criticize how I choose to treat myself.
In fact, how I choose to treat this illness, or not,
is none of your damn business?

You – who saw the *Silver Linings Playbook* – twice!
And so, you KNOW of what you speak
Your micro expertise droning on into nothingness.

And now I'm left here to curse your sudden and
    inevitable betrayal
(I'll pause here so those in the know can sigh and
    reminisce)
Because it's just too hard, it's exhausting, but I'll
    understand?

Please don't say it's for the best.
You who seem to have conveniently forgotten
in your mad dash to anywhere but here.

I didn't ask for anything. I didn't have to.
15 minutes and one heartfelt confidence ago – we were
    friends.
For you my friendship now comes with a taint.

There will be midnight phone calls.
Missing jewelery and liberties taken.
I'll ruin the wedding and destroy the marriage.

Show up uninvited and leave misery in my wake.
That's what they say. That's what you read.
You can't see past the diagnosis and it's just not worth it.

Please don't tell me that you know how I feel.

You couldn't possibly.

Medium of Release
Michael Istvan

1

Taking it out on the funeral director.

2

Weed brings them together after several years
silent since the repressed "bad touches,"
but dad's high compliments are tinged with flirtation.

3

Those who grope for the brass ring in hope that all
will then be okay, but are let down after reaching it
because death is what they were after all along.

4

If either is worthy of being wiped out,
it is not the conman but the smug one
who really thinks that he is a sorcerer.

5

People still lose themselves
in play, knowing there to be
no chance to make the NBA.

6

Mugs held between sweater sleeves at the fire.

7

Lead convulsions.

8

Yard sale prescription glasses.

9

Because the dread of death is lingering –
that is how we still manage daily tasks
with the dread of death lingering.

10

Warm baths before school
from a dish sponge dipped
in coffee pot water.

11

Condemning gay sex on grounds
that Leviticus unequivocally forbids it
even as you catch pigskin footballs.

12

Sometimes the subject
is not to be centered
in the viewfinder.

13

Condemning gay sex on grounds
that most animals do not do it
even as you use an electric toothbrush.

14

Thoughts turning hair grey.

15

Straight-razor tucked in the bra.

16

What is left in the fridge after death.

17

Breasts that can be thrown over shoulder.

18

Furrows cross the grain of the deejay's corduroys.

19

Workdays spent building with packets of sweetener.

20

Driving around all day getting pain prescriptions filled.

21

Those for whom the smaller the talk the better the buoy.

22

Not wanting to admit, even
to yourself, your hope
to die in your sleep.

23

Casual explanations
are more shaded than before –
unexpected side orders.

24

Those sentenced to be hung
forced in the meantime
to carry out hangings.

25

If to have a title on a poem
is to treat the reader as dumb,
where should the cutting stop?

26

A self-help book for how to open up to self-help books.

27

His blank face, as he bottles
the infant in his arms, speaks
of submission to his fate.

28

Bodily deformities
(goiters, humps, lop-shoulders) taken as signs of evil
character.

29

Waterways of yellow fury run
over bridges, but evacuees
first load their cars to the limit.

30

Arms-out entries from high cliffs: water-bruising.

31

Painters who seem apprenticed on separate planets.

32

A mother's bra –
booby traps
for the three-year old.

33

Avoiding each other's eyes
to deny the threat
that we have been denying.

Swan | Natalie Crick

I scrub mouse blood from the floorboards
Imagining ice,
Imagining throats.
The dead stay dead.

A necked Swan
Sits disgraced,
The pale bone poking through, a
Sword rising from a lake
Sharp and still sheathed.
The bone is so white
I could have carved
It from wax,
Soft as bees,
A candle without a flame.

Forever Winter, the sky
Looks cold, pink as a clot
In the mouth
When the lights go out.

Bosch & Keaton Hide Behind a Poem About a Deer | Jim Zola

Bosch flutters his fingers in front of his face
Buster hides behind a bowtie disguise
I once watched a man fly
over my car
late at night
on route 28A
heading back to Falmouth
So drunk
he stood up
and stared at me
mouth open
He became a deer
running back into the woods
pine brush and nettles
The artist crosses himself
The actor moons

A Fire Without Light #493
Darren Demaree

He is convinced we need a great storm. All I see is a hundred downed trees, and a distinct absence of song. Because every nest is fragile, we dare not kneel to anyone within our own spit and comfort.

A Fire Without Light #494
Darren Demaree

Lift the foil length from the center. Let the air at him.
If he goes bad quickly the smell might just un-elect
him. Leave him on the counter. Let's see what happens.
We can always just burn this house down.

A Fire Without Light #495
Darren Demaree

This is the same Ohio it's always been. We're a project. We're Jesus and a prayer. We've never really taken responsibility for anything. I can't talk anyone in my family into admitting that they can run without the wind of God. I think it's all so lovely when there are celebrations, but the rest of the time these people are too damn weak to do much about anything.

Forward | James Croal Jackson

Your son
has no teeth
in his exit.

Junipers sprout
along the edges
of the street.

A tomato grows
in your garden
of the fertile.

Dust and ice
compose the rings
of Saturn.

What else is there?
Cries long lost
in the stars.

Glass Alibi | Charles Kell

It's in the evidence strewn
about. Ripped & written,
the open block drags
us back to the broken smoke scene.

You can still blame the black weather.
The late way I dragged you
kicking & screaming from
that sick junk cell. Together,

we rode toward the rip tide.
In a far off city your third eye
caught the last half shape paralyzed
in the doorway. Two coats, keys,

ring of skin trapped fast in a back
memory. There was your mouth
shining red just before dawn.
You broke the window & took

off. Closing my eyes was easy.

Summer is a Dream
Gary Sokolow

There were explosions over sky, I
    had heard of the bomb makers
behind stone walls, as I rise from this bed
    as others try but can't and decide
I can be anyone, anywhere, doing anything.

I write of the most intimate things: a wicker
    basket moved under a desk, the steam
radiator too hot throughout winter. Here I play
    at nothing, am content to watch a summer
storm dump three inches of rain, drown the azaleas,
    threaten to wash away some town deep
in the heart of Jersey.

Here it all seems so easy: the woman on the screen
    in a sparkling dress, the official waving behind
a phalanx of security. Easy. Like the ache of love for
    the dark haired woman, her beauty, a mirage,
dissolving into the scorching heat of a July noon.

recipes | Mark Young

#1

Take on the
words of others

& then take
out the words

you do not
like. Whatever

is left is right.

2

Take ~~on~~ the
words of others

& then take
~~out~~ the words

you ~~do not~~
like. Whatever

~~is left~~ is right.

Near Miss | Robert Stout

We lurch against each other,
transformed by rain
into lone survivors
whose fingers clutch hard edges
as traffic screeches past,
gravel spatters the axles
and the front seat fills with the smell
of scorched tires and burning brakes.

                                      Then continue,

slowly, a colt behind us
racing its shadow and the rain
washing our reflections
down separate
window panes.

Dear Ron | Bart Solarczyk

So far it's six beers
& six Sicilian slices could get better if you
float me six green clouds.

Catherine Arra is the author of *Slamming & Splitting* (Red Ochre Press 2014), *Loving from the Backbone* (Flutter Press 2015) and forthcoming in 2017, *Tales of Intrigue & Plumage* (FutureCycle Press). She lives in the Hudson Valley in upstate New York. Find her at www.catherinearra.com

Ron Androla has been writing & publishing since the 1970s. He's the author of *Confluence* (Busted Dharma Books) 2015, *Factory Fables* (Pressure Press) 2016, & many more books, available on Amazon. He lives in Erie, PA with his wife, Ann Androla.

Megan Bell is a displaced Pittsburgh-native, living on the edge of Cayuga Lake. She enjoys levitating, wearing as few clothes as possible at any given time, & drinking gin neat. Maybe a lime. She is currently in a Master of Science program for Acupuncture & Chinese internal medicine.

Robert Beveridge makes noise (http://www.xterminal.bandcamp.com) and writes poetry just outside Cleveland, OH. He went through a messy divorce with Facebook some months ago, and as a result his relationship with time is much improved. Recent/upcoming appearances in *Ghost*

City Review, *Minor Literature[s]*, and *Barking Sycamores*, among others.

Heidi Blakeslee has been writing poetry for 22yrs. She's published a memoir, *The White Cat*, a novel, *Strange Man: The Edgar Allan Foe*, and two poetry books, *The Empress of Hours*, and *Should the Need Arise: Poems*. She is the founder of the "Poetry in the Park" festival, which ran for four years in Erie, Pa. She currently lives in Pittsburgh with her longtime partner James Trevison and her seven cats.

S.E. Clark is a proud graduate of Lesley University's MFA program. Her work has appeared in *Rose Red Review*, *Geek Force Five*, *The Drum Magazine* and *Lady Churchill's Rosebud Wristlet*. She lives in a small town outside of Boston, Massachusetts, where she collects folklore and forages through old cemeteries for names.

Natalie Crick, from the UK, has found delight in writing all of her life and first began writing when she was a very young girl. Her poetry has been published or is forthcoming in a range of journals and magazines including *Ink in Thirds, The Penwood Review, Interpreters House,*

The Chiron Review and *Rust + Moth*. Her work also features or is forthcoming in a number of anthologies, including Lehigh Valley Vanguard Collections 13.

The author of six poetry collections, most recently *Many Full Hands Applauding Inelegantly* (8th House Publishing) and the Managing Editor of the Best of the Net Anthology and Ovenbird Poetry, **Darren Demaree's** poems have appeared, or are scheduled to appear in numerous magazines/journals, including the *South Dakota Review, Meridian, New Letters, Diagram*, and the *Colorado Review*. He lives in Columbus, Ohio with his wife and children.

Angela Dragani is a poet by day, auditor by night. She is currently working on material for a book of poetry highlighting those who suffer from mental illness, as she herself has Bipolar 1. Born in Vancouver, she spent many years in Nunavut and Nunatsiavut before settling in Nova Scotia.

Daniel Fitzpatrick grew up in New Orleans and now lives in Hot Springs, Arkansas, with his wife and daughter. His poems have appeared in several journals, including *2River View, Coe Review*, and *Panoplyzine*. In addition to writing, he enjoys kayaking the Diamond Lakes, micro-farming, and exploring the Ouachita Mountains.

Mark DeCarteret's work has appeared next to Charles Bukowski in a lo-fi fold out, Pope John Paul II in a high test collection of Catholic poetry, Billy Collins in an Italian fashion coffee table book, and Mary Oliver in a 3785 page pirated anthology.

R.M. Engelhardt is a veteran poet-writer currently living in Troy NY whose work over the years has been published in such journals & magazines as *Poetic Diversity. Rusty Truck, Sure! The Charles Bukowski Newsletter, Thunder Sandwich, Red Fez, Full of Crow, 2nd Ave Poetry* and in many others. His new book of poems is *The Bones of Our Existence, Poems 2046* **www.thepoemremains.com**

Howie Good is the author of *Dangerous Acts Starring Unstable Elements*, winner of the 2015 Press Americana Prize. His latest books are *A Ghost Sings, a Door Opens from Another New Calligraphy* and *Robots vs. Kung Fu* from AngelHouse Press.

Richard D. Houff has had new writing published in *Beatnik Cowboy, Chiron Review, Homestead Review*, and *Misfit*. His latest book of poems, *Night Watch and Other Hometown Favorites* was published by Black Cat Moon Press.

Nancy Iannucci is a historian who teaches history and lives poetry in Troy, NY. Her work is published/forthcoming in numerous publications including *Bop Dead City, Star 82 Review, Gargoyle, Amaryllis, Typehouse Literary Magazine, Autumn Sky Poetry Daily, Poetry Breakfast, Rose Red Review*, and *Three Drops from a Cauldron*. Her poem, HOWLING, won *Yellow Chair Review's* Rock the Chair Challenge.

Mark Jackley's work has appeared in *Fifth Wednesday, Sugar House Review, Natural Bridge* and other journals. His new book of poems *On the Edge of a Very Small Town* is available for free at chineseplums@gmail.com.

James Croal Jackson is the author of *The Frayed Edge of Memory* (Writing Knights Press, 2017). His poetry has appeared in *The Bitter Oleander, Rust + Moth, Cosmonauts Avenue*, and elsewhere. He has won the William Redding Memorial Poetry Contest and been a finalist for the Princemere Poetry Prize. Find him in Columbus, Ohio or at jimjakk.com.

Seth Jani currently resides in Seattle, WA and is the founder of Seven CirclePress. His own work has been published widely in such places as *The Chiron Review, Inscape, El Portal, The Hamilton Stone Review, Hawai`i Pacific Review, VAYAVYA, Gingerbread House* and *Gravel*. Visit him at www.sethjani.com.

Emma Johnson-Rivard is a Masters student at Hamline University. She received her undergraduate degree in Film Studies at Smith College in Massachusetts and currently lives in Minnesota with her dogs and far too many books. Her work has appeared in *Mistake House, the Olive Press*, and *the Moon City Press*.

Sam Landry is completely lost and wants to know where a good place to get pizza is around here. He is a Pushcart Prize nominee for his work published in *Outlook Springs*, along with his self-publishing on his Magic cards website turnonemagic.com. In his free time he awaits death in Gloucester, MA.

Taylor Liljegran is a poet and educator based in the Greater Boston area. She released her first chapbook *The Sessions: Lucy Ricardo Talks to Her Therapist* in 2014. Her work is also included in the anthology *Best Indie Lit New England: Vol. 2* (Black Key Press 2015).

Clare L. Martin's second collection of poetry, *Seek the Holy Dark*, is forthcoming from Yellow Flag Press in 2017. Her acclaimed debut collection of poetry, *Eating the Heart First*, was published by Press 53. Martin's poetry has appeared in *Thrush Poetry Journal*, *Melusine*, *Poets and Artists*, and *Louisiana Literature*, among others.

Corey Mesler has published in numerous journals including *Poetry* and *Esquire*. He has published novels, short story collections, chapbooks, and 4 full-length poetry collections. He's been nominated for many Pushcarts, and 2 of his poems were chosen for Garrison Keillor's Writer's Almanac. He runs a bookstore in Memphis.

Gloria Mindock is editor of Cervena Barva Press and a USA editor for Levure Litteraire (France). Her fourth book of poetry, *Whiteness of Bone*, was published by

Glass Lyre Press in 2016. Her poetry has been translated and published into the Romanian, Spanish, Estonian, French, Bosnian, Croatian, Serbian, and Montenegrin.

Kurt Nimmo is a long-time small press veteran, the editor of *The Smudge Review* in the 1970s and *Planet Detroit* in the 1980s. He lives in Las Cruces, New Mexico, with his wife and cat.

Lee Okan is an editor's assistant at Macmillan Learning. She graduated from Lesley University, MFA creative writing.

Elissa Rashkin is a research professor in Communication and Cultural Studies at the Universidad Veracruzana in Mexico. Author of books and articles on Mexican cultural history, along with artisanal poetry and fiction chapbooks published by Pas de Chance Press of Toronto.

Zvi A. Sesling is the Brookline, MA Poet Laureate. He edits Muddy River Poetry Review. He has published two books of poetry *Fire Tongue* (Cervena Barva, 2016), *King of the Jungle* (Ibbetson Street, 2010) and two chapbooks *Love Poems From Hell* (Flutter Press, 2017) and *Across Stones of Bad Dreams* (Cervena Barva, 2011).

Gary Sokolow has a long ago MFA from Brooklyn College, lives in NYC, and has been published in *Chantarelle's Notebook, Blood Lotus Review*, and *Up the Staircase Quarterly*.

Bart Solarczyk lives in Pittsburgh, PA. His 9th chapbook, *Right Direction*, was recently published by Lilliput Review as part of the Modest Proposal series.

Robert Joe Stout's most recent books are *Monkey Screams* and *Where Gringos Don't Belong*. Other books include *A Perfect Throw* (Aldrich Press), *Hidden Dangers* (Sunbury Press) and *Running Out the Hurt* (Kindle). He is a freelance journalist who has written for a variety of magazines, including *New Politics*. Born in Nebraska, he now lives in Oaxaca, Mexico.

Belinda Subraman has been writing poetry since the 6th grade and publishing since college. She had a ten year run editing and publishing *Gypsy Literary Magazine*. Six of those ten years was from Germany where she was a Bohemian outcast among officer wives. She edited books by Vergin' Press, among them: Henry Miller and My Big Sur Days by Judson Crews.

Aden Thomas grew up in central Wyoming. Previously his work has been featured in *The Kentucky Review*, *The Inflectionist Review*, and *The Chiron Review*. He lives north of Denver, Colorado.

Tim Suermondt is the author of three full-length collections of poems: *Trying To Help The Elephant Man Dance* (The Backwaters Press, 2007), *Just Beautiful* (New York Quarterly Books, 2010) and *Election Night And The Five Satins* (Glass Lyre Press, 2016) — along with three chapbooks. He has poems published in *Poetry, The Georgia Review, Ploughshares, Prairie Schooner, Blackbird, Bellevue Literary Review, North Dakota Quarterly, december magazine, Plume Poetry Journal, Poetry East* and *Stand Magazine* (England), among others.

Mark Young's most recent books are *Ley Lines* & *bricolage*, both from gradient books of Finland, *The Chorus of the Sphinxes*, from Moria Books in Chicago, & *some more strange meteorites*, from Meritage & i.e. Press, California / New York.

Jim Zola has worked in a warehouse, as a security guard, in a bookstore, as a teacher for Deaf children, as a toy designer for Fisher Price, and currently as a children's librarian. Published in many journals through the years, his publications include a chapbook – *The One Hundred Bones of Weather* (Blue Pitcher Press) – and a full length poetry collection – *What Glorious Possibilities* (Aldrich Press). He currently lives in Greensboro, NC

Nixes Mate Books features small-batch artisanal literature, created by writers that use all 26 letters of the alphabet and then some, honing their craft the time-honored way: one line at a time.

More Nixes Mate titles:

ON BROAD SOUND | Rusty Barnes
KINKY KEEPS THE HOUSE CLEAN | Mari Deweese
SQUALL LINE ON THE HORIZON | Pris Campbell
COMES TO THIS | Jeff Weddle
HITCHHIKING BEATITUDES | Michael McInnis
AIR & OTHER STORIES | Lauren Leja
WAITING FOR AN ANSWER | Heather Sullivan
A WORLD WHERE | Paul Brookes
MY SOUTHERN CHILDHOOD | Pris Campbell
THE PAUL BUNYAN BALLROOM | Bud Backen
THE WILLOW HOWL | Lisa Brognano
CAPP ROAD | Matt Borczon

Forthcoming titles from Nixes Mate:

LUBBOCK ELECTRIC | Anne Elezabeth Pluto
STARLAND | Jessica Purdy
JESUS IN THE GHOST ROOM | Rusty Barnes
HEART OF THE BROKEN WORLD | Jeff Weddle
SMOKEY OF THE MIGRAINES | Michael McInnis
SHE NEEDS THAT EDGE | Paul Brookes
LABOR | Lisa DeSiro
HE WAS A GOOD FATHER | Mark Borczon

nixesmate.pub/books

www.ingramcontent.com/pod-product-compliance
Lightning Source LLC
Chambersburg PA
CBHW050541300426
44113CB00012B/2205